Poems about

Homes

**Selected by
Amanda Earl & Danielle Sensier**

**Illustrated by
Frances Lloyd**

Wayland

Titles in the series
Poems about . . .

Animals	**Food**
Colours	**Growth**
Day & Night	**Homes**
Families	**Journeys**
Feelings	**Weather**

For Josephine

Series editor: Catherine Baxter
Designer: Loraine Hayes

First published in 1994 by
Wayland (Publishers) Ltd
61 Western Road, Hove
East Sussex BN3 1JD, England

Typeset by Dorchester Typesetting
Group Ltd., Dorset, England.
Printed and bound in Italy by
G. Canale & C.S.p.A., Turin.

British Library Cataloguing in Publication Data

Poems About Homes. – (Poems About . . . Series)
 I. Earl, Amanda II. Sensier, Danielle
 III. Series
 808.819355

ISBN 0–7502–1124–5

Front cover design S. Balley

Poets' nationalities

Shel Silverstein	American
Doug Macleod	Australian
Patricia Maria Tan	Asian
Myra Cohn Livingston	American
Danielle Vasse	English
Miroslav Holub	Czech
Jack Prelutsky	American
James Reeves	English
Nikki Giovanni	Afro-American
Mary Coleridge	English
Joseph Dewar	English
Chief Seattle	Northwest Indian

Contents

Tree House

A tree house, a free house,
A secret you and me house,
A high up in the leafy branches
Cozy as can be house.

A street house, a neat house,
Be sure and wipe your feet house
Is not my kind of house at all –
Let's go live in a tree house.

Shel Silverstein

Thank You, Dad, for Everything

Thank you for laying the carpet, Dad,
Thank you for showing us how,
But what is that lump in the middle, Dad?
And why is it saying mia-ow?

Doug Macleod

6

Into the Kitchen

Into the kitchen
Sulin goes
With a chicken
And potatoes.

She puts some water
Into a pot
Then she waits
Until it's hot.

Into the pot
She puts the chicken,
While it cooks
The soup will thicken.

She adds the potatoes
And stirs the pot,
When everything's cooked
She'll eat it hot.

Patricia Maria Tan

8

Home

Snow in the air tonight,
Roads freeze:
No birds sing, cold trees,
But the kitchen is warm, bright.

Leonard Clark

Buildings

Buildings are a great surprise,
Every one's a different size.

Offices
grow
long
and high,
tall
enough
to
touch
the
sky.

Houses seem
more like a box,
made of glue
and building blocks.

Every time you look, you see
Buildings shaped quite differently.

Myra Cohn Livingston

Sad

Why so sad I ask myself?
For all the people out on the streets,
Why so sad I ask myself?
No home, no money, no love,
Why so sad I ask myself?
Could we love? Could we care? Could we
give to everyone?
Why so sad I ask myself?

Sad!!   Sad!!
Why so bad?

Danielle Vasse (child poet)

Fairy Tale

He built himself a house,
    his foundations,
    his stones,
    his walls,
    his roof overhead,
    his chimney and smoke,
    his view from the window.

He made himself a garden,
    his fence
    his thyme,
    his earthworm,
    his evening dew.

He cut out his bit of sky above.

And he wrapped the garden in the sky
and the house in the garden
and packed the lot in a handkerchief
and went off
lone as an arctic fox
through the cold
unending
rain
into the world.

Miroslav Holub
(translated from Czech by George Theiner)

Home! You're Where It's Warm Inside

Home! You are a special place;
you're where I wake and wash my face,
brush my teeth and comb my hair,
change my socks and underwear,
clean my ears and blow my nose,
try on all my parents' clothes.

Home! You're where it's warm inside,
where my tears are gently dried,
where I'm comforted and fed,
where I'm forced to go to bed,
where there's always love to spare;
Home! I'm glad that you are there.

Jack Prelutsky

17

The snail

At sunset, when the night-dews fall,
Out of the ivy on the wall
With horns outstretched and pointed tail
Comes the grey and noiseless snail.
On ivy stems she clambers down,
Carrying her house of brown.
Safe in the dark, no greedy eye
Can her tender body spy,
While she herself, a hungry thief,
Searches out the freshest leaf.
She travels on as best she can
Like a toppling caravan.

James Reeves

Snail

Snail upon the wall,
Have you got at all
Anything to tell
About your shell?

Only this, my child –
When the wind is wild,
Or when the sun is hot,
It's all I've got.

John Drinkwater

from **The Bed Book**

BEDS come in all sizes –
Single or double,
Cot-size or cradle,
King-size or trundle.

Most Beds are Beds
For sleeping or resting,
But the best Beds are much
More interesting!

Not just a white little
Tucked-in-tight little
Nighty-night little
Turn-out-the-light little
 Bed –

 Instead
A Bed for Fishing,
A Bed for Cats,
A Bed for a Troupe of
 Acrobats.

The right sort of Bed
(if you see what I mean)
Is a Bed that might
Be a Submarine.

Nosing through water
Clear and green,
Silver and glittery
As a sardine.

Or a Jet-Propelled Bed
For visiting Mars
With mosquito nets
For the shooting stars . . .

Sylvia Plath

The new neighbour

Have you had your tonsils out?
    Do you go to school?
Do you know that there are frogs
    Down by the Willow Pool?

Are you good at cricket?
    Have you got a bat?
Do you know the proper way
    To feed a white rat?

Are there any apples
    On your apple tree?
Do you think your mother
    Will ask me in to tea?

Rose Fyleman

Covers

Glass covers windows
   to keep the cold away
Clouds cover the sky
   to make a rainy day

Night time covers
   all the things that creep
Blankets cover me
   when I'm asleep

Nikki Giovanni

When All the World's Asleep

Where do insects go at night,
When all the world's asleep?
Where do bugs and butterflies
And caterpillars creep?
Turtles sleep inside their shells;
The robin has her nest.
Rabbits and the sly old fox
Have holes where they can rest.
Bears can crawl inside a cave;
The lion has his den.
Cows can sleep inside the barn,
And pigs can use their pen.
But where do bugs and butterflies
And caterpillars creep,
When everything is dark outside
And all the world's asleep.

Anita E. Posey

The deserted house

There's no smoke in the chimney,
And the rain beats on the floor;
There's no glass in the window,
There's no wood in the door;
The heather grows behind the house,
And the sand lies before.

No hand hath trained the ivy,
The walls are grey and bare;
The boats upon the sea sail by,
Nor ever tarry there.
No beast of the field comes nigh,
Nor any bird of the air.

Mary Coleridge

Leaf's Lament

No-one cares about me,
A leaf hanging high in the tree.
They care about monkeys and things
And parrots with beautiful wings,
that squawk and shout
And fly about

And look at the beautiful things.

The place where I usually am
is now being destroyed by man
Who chops down the wood,
and does me no good
And kills all the things that I am.

Joseph Dewar (child poet)

from **Brother Eagle, Sister Sky**

. . . Preserve the land and the air and the rivers for your children's children and love it as we have loved it.

Chief Seattle

How to use this book

Poetry is a very enjoyable area of literature and children take to it naturally, usually beginning with nursery rhymes. It's what happens next that can make all the difference! This series of thematic poetry anthologies keeps poetry alive and enjoyable for young children.

When using these books there are several ways in which you can help a child to appreciate poetry and to understand the ways in which words can be carefully chosen and sculpted to convey different atmospheres and meanings. Try to encourage the following:

- Joining in when the poem is read out loud.
- Talking about favourite words, phrases or images.
- Discussing the illustration and photographs.
- Miming facial expressions to suit the mood of the poems.
- Acting out events in the poems.
- Copying out the words.
- Learning favourite poems by heart.
- Discussing the difference between a poem and a story.
- Clapping hands to rhythmic poems.
- Talking about metaphors/similes eg what kind of weather would a lion be? What colour would sadness be? What would it taste like? If you could hold it, how would it feel?

It is inevitable that, at some point, children will want to write poems themselves. Writing a poem is, however, only one way of enjoying poetry. With the above activities, children can be encouraged to appreciate and delight in this unique form of communication.

Picture acknowledgements

Ace 17 (T & J Sims), 26 (Rafael Macia), 28/29 (Peter Adams); A P M
cover; Life File 4/5 (Jeremy Hoare); Robert Harding 19; Skjold 12;
Tony Stone Worldwide 10 (Bob Kirst), 24 (Bill Truslow); WPL 22.

Text acknowledgements

For permission to reprint copyright material the publishers gratefully
acknowledge the following: Faber & Faber Limited for an extract
from *'The Bed Book'* by Sylvia Plath. Reprinted by permission of the
publisher; John Johnson Limited for 'The Snail' from *'The Wandering
Moon'* by James Reeves. Copyright © 1950 The Estate of James
Reeves. Published by William Heinemann Ltd; Brian Lee for 'Sad . . .
and Glad'. Reprinted by permission of the author; Marian Reiner for
'Buildings' from *'Whispers and Other Poems'* by Myra Cohn
Livingston. Copyright © 1958, 1986 Myra Cohn Livingston. Reprinted
by permission of Marian Reiner for the author; Danielle Vasse for
'Sad'. Reprinted by permission of the author. While every effort has
been made to secure permission, in some cases it has proved impossi-
ble to trace the copyright holders. The publishers apologise for this
apparent negligence.

Index of first lines